TABLE OF CONTENTS

Introduction

British Library Cataloguing-in-Publication Data. A catalogue record for
this book is available from the British Library.

Tight Lacing
A Bilbliography of articles and letters concerning
Stays and Corsets for men and women
Part I 1828-1880

© 1999 Peter Farrer

ISBN 0 9512385 8 2

Published by Karn Publications Garston
63 Salisbury Road, Garston, Liverpool L19 0PH

Design by Vivienne Palfreyman
Printed in England by Saints & Co Ltd, Liverpool

Cover illustration:
PLANCHE XII Corset Leoty (1867) from Le Corset A Travers Les Ages,
Ernest Leoty (Paris: Paul Ollendorff, 1893)

INTRODUCTION

In 1949 my attention was drawn to the correspondence in *The Englishwoman's Domestic Magazine* by Doris Langley Moore's *The Woman in Fashion*. I was particularly intrigued by the reference to men wearing stays. As I was up at Oxford at the time I was able to go straight to the Bodleian and consult the relevant volumes myself. Since then I have discovered a whole series of newspapers and magazines continuing up to 1941 which contain correspondence about the wearing of stays and corsets by either sex.

In the eighteenth century medical writers condemned the body-restricting corsets of the time. When the fashionable shape again required a narrow waist in the second quarter of the nineteenth century, the medical attack was renewed, with this difference in Britain. The popular Press was not simply content to print the diatribes of the doctors in the form of medical articles, it also allowed the ordinary stay-wearer to express her (or his) opinion in the form of a letter to the editor. In the period under review three newspapers or magazines in particular gave space to this subject, either over a period of time or in short bursts. They were: *The Family Herald*, *The Queen* and *The Englishwoman's Domestic Magazine*.

The editor of *The Family Herald* was opposed to tight-lacing, although he appreciated that fashion required a distinct emphasis on a small waist, so he realised that not much could be done about it, but he was happy to print letters from women who had "given up" stays . His normal method was to quote part of a letter and then give a reply, that is, he provided an "Answer" to a correspondent, in a whimsical or serious manner as he thought fit. Sometimes, however, a letter was quoted in full. When the owners of *The Field* acquired *The Queen* in 1862, they introduced correspondence columns on a variety of subjects on the lines of those in the former paper. Letters were printed in full and readers replied to each other's letters. The narrow waist came up for discussion and letters were printed from 1862 to 1866. This led to a little booklet called *The Corset Defended* being published in 1865. Samuel Beeton invited readers' contributions from the first issue of *The Englishwoman's Domestic Magazine* in 1852. At first he followed the practice of *The Family Herald* and commented on the letters. From 1867 he printed letters in full, and gave his readers complete freedom to express their views. All three papers were concerned with women's interests and family matters, so it was natural that such topics as domestic discipline and tight-lacing should come up, especially as all three accepted revelations of a personal or even intimate nature. I might add that the readers of *The Family Herald* were also keenly interested in religion and theology.

As an editor and publisher, Beeton was very responsive to his public. Readers wrote to him and in the course of his career he exploited their contributions in three notable ways. First, readers' recipes were included in Mrs. Beeton's *The Book of Household Management* (1861). Then, surplus letters on corporal punishment were printed in monthly supplements to *The Englishwoman's Domestic Magazine* from April to December 1870 inclusive. Meanwhile, some of the corset letters, together with some from *The Queen* and other material, were reprinted in a book, *The Corset and the Crinoline*, in 1868. Two further books were published soon after, one, the anti-corset *Madre Natura versus The Moloch of Fashion* by Chatto & Windus in 1870 and another collection of letters, *Figure Training*, by Ward, Lock and Tyler, in 1871.

The purpose of these notes is to list the letters which appeared in the three papers together with other letters and articles in other papers within the period; to summarise the four books mentioned and finally to show the interconnection between the books and the letters and to show which letters were reprinted in which book. In this connection I have included only periodicals or books published in the U.K. Both David Kunzle in *Fashion and Fetishism* and Valerie Steele in *Fashion and Eroticism*, published in 1982 and 1985 respectively, describe and discuss this correspondence and place it within the context of the full range of American and European as well as U.K. sources. Both discovered references unknown to me, which I acknowledge where appropriate.

I have carried out my research in The British Library, The British Newspaper Library, Colindale, North London, The Bodleian, The Victoria and Albert Museum, Liverpool Public Library and especially at The Gallery of Costume, Platt Hall, Rusholme, Manchester, and I thank all the Keepers, from Anne Buck to Anthea Jarvis, for their help.

The Family Herald is available in The British Newspaper Library, and in The Bodleian. There are some volumes in the Cambridge University Library and in Birmingham Central Library. *The Queen* may be seen at The British Newspaper Library. *E.D.M.* is held by several Libraries: The British Library, The Bodleian, Cambridge University, Victoria & Albert Museum, Liverpool John Moores University and Birmingham. The holdings of these libraries in detail may be ascertained from *The British Union Catalogue of Periodicals*. *The Queen* and *E.D.M.* may also be consulted by appointment at The Gallery of Costume, Platt Hall.

Peter Farrer
1999

Notes

(nos.)   Nos. in brackets below dates indicate issue number

p/c   Photocopies available

	Vol.	Date	Page		

1 Source not known

1828 — "A letter from a tradesman" complaining about daughters squeezing their waists.
Cited by Dr. C. Willett Cunningdon in *Feminine Attitudes in the Nineteenth Century* (London: Heinemann, 1935) p59
no reference given
mentioned by Kunzle, p134

2 The Penny Magazine

2 — 28/2/1833 — 77-80 — "On the ill effects of Insufficient exercise, Constrained Positions, and Tight Stays, on the Health of Young Women".
Cited in Poole & Fletcher. Referred to by Frank Buckland in a letter to *The Queen*, 15/8/1863. p115

3 The Ladies Pocket Magazine

March 1837 — 107-8 — Review of William Coulson, *On Deformities of the Chest* (London: Thomas Hurst, 1836)
Cited by Janet Dunbar, *The Early Victorian Woman* (London: Harrap, 1953)

4 Provincial Medical and Surgical

(started 3.10.1840, from 1853 continued as *The British Medical Journal*)

I — 6.11.1841 — 110 — "Compression of the Female Waist by Stays." Report by J. Nottingham, a Liverpool doctor, on dead body woman aged 23.
Kunzle 349. This is in the the third half- yearly volume, but, for some reason, has been renumbered I.

5 The Family Herald [commenced 13.5.1842]

Miscellaneous short paragraphs about the dangers of tight-lacing: Photocopies taken of longer letters and articles.

II — 31.8.1844 — 268 — Girl aged 20 died: – stooped – addicted to the dangerous practice of tight-lacing.

7.12.1844 — 492 — Quotes from *Medical Times* penalties of tight-lacing

21.12.1844 — 524 — K.O.H.L. writes: stocks, cravats, stays: why do we do it?

18.1.1845 — 587 — more from *Medical Times*

III — 13.12.1845 — 507 — ADVERT:
"Ladies Tight-lacing Superseded by Easy Fitting, Fashionable made Stays: Mrs. C. Stent, 24, Guildford Place, Wilmington Square.
"To the making Young Ladies' and Children's Stays Mrs. Stent devotes a special care".

7.3.1846 (148) — 700 — FAMILY MATTERS:
Editor quotes a question from Q.P.X.V.: how can stays be avoided? has infant daughter. Then gives answer from a "matron", to whom he referred the question:
"Q.P.X.V. will find that if she never uses her daughter to stays they will never be required. I have known instances in which girls have worn no stays (at least not *boned* stays) up to age of ten or eleven years; and if they could do without them until then, they could surely do without them altogether. …if required, a piece of jean, quarter-yard deep, with a few cottons stitched in it, would answer every purpose. These were the only stays worn by the children to whom I have alluded above." E.W.

IV — 1.8.1946 — 204 — Tight-lacing: cites comment of doctor that it is a public benefit, as it kills off the foolish girls.

Vol.	Date	Page	
V	21.8.1847 (224)	253	FAMILY MATTERS: Tight-lacing causes red noses.

V — 21.8.1847 (224) — 253 — FAMILY MATTERS:
Tight-lacing causes red noses.

20.11.1847 (237) — 458 — HEPHISBA:
We cannot tell 'how to keep the waist in a desirable form without stays, corsets, buckling of belts, waistbands or girdles', if Nature has not made it so. The fashionable waist is unnatural, and certainly not like the waist of the marble models of Greece.

4.3.1848 (252) — 700 — SIZE OF THE FEMALE WAIST
'Women ought to measure from 27 to 29 inches round the waist; but most females do not permit themselves to grow beyond twenty-four; thousands are laced to twenty-one, some to less than twenty inches; and thus by means of wood, whalebone and steel, the chest is often reduced to one-half its proper size'.   Apparently a quotation, but the source is not given.

18.3.1848 (254) — 732 — ORIGIN OF STAYS:
Ascribed to invention of a brutal butcher of the 13th century as a punishment for a loquacious wife. Other husbands followed him until it became a fashion.

1.4.1848 (256) — 764 — THE FEMALE WAIST:
Dear Mr. Editor, – In No. 252 you state that the female waist ought to measure from 27 to 29 inches round. Now I am rather stout, and wear no stays; still I only measure 23 inches; indeed, I am considered to have a very thick waist; so pray say in your next if you have made a mistake in the figures. By doing so you will greatly oblige
NO FLIRT
(There is no mistake in the figures. There are few matrons whose waists do not exceed the admeasurement given. Those of maidens are unnaturally compressed, as they prefer sacrificing health to fashion; but marriage soon spoils a fine waist.)

V — 22.4.1848 (259) — 810 — EVELINA: says her waist measures 26 inches, though she is only 16; whilst another lady this week says hers measures only 22½, though she has had four children. Our little paragraph upon waists has been severely criticised.

29.4.1848 (260) — 826 — LILY: Tight-lacing no harm if not done to excess: has worn stays all her life: suggests Editor should try a pair (of men's stays): other comments on bustles, shoes. Editor agrees lacing only injurious when 'it forces nature'.   p/c

VI — 13.5.1848 (262) — 25 — MASSY MAGPIE: has lately taken a great dislike to stays and wants to know how she can provide a substitute for them. – impossible unless adopt Grecian dress, but our climate unfavourable – Those accustomed to stays should not abandon, but avoid tightness etc.   p/c

3.6.1848 (265) — 74 — CANARY BIRD: is disappointed with our answer to LUCY, and thinks stays unnecessary: – the round and small waist suited to present style of dress, which is artificial. To restore waist to natural shape, fashion must change.

LUCRETIA: says she does not wear stays, but a simple boddice [*sic*], made of jean: – this is a pair of stays. p/c

75 THE FEMALE WAIST.
GREENWICH: The measurement of the waist given in No. 252 has been confirmed as the proper general size by many who have the best opportunities of judging. No sensible girl will envy our fair correspondent her waist of 18 inches, since it appears impossible that the lungs and viscera can have room to perform their functions in so small a space.

17.6.1848 (267)   105   ISABELLA G: left off stays to please her husband
p/c

24.6.1848 (268)   122   ROSY CHEEK: Doctors will complain that your campaign against tight-lacing will reduce business.

HERMINIE: she is 5' 2", never wears stays, waist is 19" invites Editor's opinion on waists which he gives at some length: admires natural shape – cannot be improved by force – quotes old lady with slender figure – never wore stays – nor her daughters. Herminie's proportions depend on width of shoulders.

SNAILIOLA: has heard that in grandmother's time stays were fastened with tapes not laces. Asks how it is done as it takes her 2½ hours to dress and is shortly to be married.
"Leave them off". p/c

29.7.1848 (273)   201   THE GIPSY: is quite correct in her ideas respecting the danger of leaving off stays, after being accustomed to wear them; and we have more than once administered the caution. It is rather in behalf of the rising generation than of adults that the anti-stay doctrine is inculcated.

26.8.1848 (277)   265   AUGUSTA M: asks what are the dangers of leaving off stays: she is 19 and stopped 6 weeks ago. The only effect so far is "that my dresses crease rather in the back." The only danger is in catching cold: thinks AUGUSTA must look more slender and elegant without her stays. p/c

11.11.1848 (288)   445-6   HINTS ON THE PRESENTATION OF HEALTH No. 10 clothing continued:
Second half of article is about tight-lacing: medical warnings in vain; corset makes the figure ugly; sudden abandonment not advised; Mr. HARE has suggested an improvement. p/c

23.12.1848 (294)   537   LOCASTRIA: seems to have been little squeezed with stays. Let her remain so in spite of the criticism of her friends. p/c

Vol.	Date	Page		
	20.1.1849 (298)	602	GEORGINA C: Editor comments on reasons for the differences of opinion about waists by artists and ladies. ...Nature at variance with fashion. Also colder climate requires more clothes. p/c	
	27.1.1849 (299)	618	J. B. In Mr Hare's work on *Spinal Deformities* will be found the information respecting improvement in the construction of the corset.	This is *Facts and observations on the Physical Education of Children especially as regards the Prevention of Spinal and other Deformities* by Samuel Hare FRCS, (London: J. Churchill 1852): illustrations of "Non-Compression Corsets" appear on pages 42-43.
	10.2.1849 (301)	651	A NORTH COUNTRY LASS: our strictures were directed against tight-lacing, not against slack-lacing. We recommend you to wear a light pair of stays, constructed according to Mr. Hare's suggestion, contained in *'Hints on Health'*, in No. 288.	
	17.2.1849 (302)	666	JANE ANNE: asks whether to take up stays again: gave up to please husband, but female friends criticise. Editor sympathises with her desire to follow fashion. p/c	
	3.3.1849 (304)	698	MARIANNE F: Her letter complaining about 'elastic' stays printed in full without comment. p/c	
	10.3.1849 (305)	714	OLIVIA: says that she is one of the emancipated fair. She has left off wearing the strait-waistcoat, and she thinks it will be a long time before she takes to stays again. But she has been obliged to dispense with peaks to her dresses, and wears round waists, with a band and buckle. JANE ANNE, of a former number has therefore, no occasion to fear being like nobody else. The emancipation is going on gradually.	
VII	12.5.1849 (314)	26	GEORGIANA, STAYS: long letter printed in full about how she gave up stays: she wears a white jean bodice. p/c	
	15.12.1849 (345)	522	ELLEN R: A staymaker – protests against press attacks on stays: Editor says the ladies are too powerful p/c	
IX	13.9.1851 (436)	317	FASHIONS FOR SEPTEMBER: From Berger's *Ladies Gazette of Fashion* para at end: Tight-lacing is completely gone out of fashion amongst *ladies* in the higher and middle classes, who have discovered that undue compression is destructive of both grace and symmetry. It is amongst young females *of the humbler classes* that the practice is now most prevalent.	
	6.3.1852 (461)	717	STAYS USEFUL ON SOME OCCASIONS AFTER ALL: Queen of Spain saved by dagger striking on whalebone.	
X	12.6.1852 (475)	106	LOLA A: is told by a lady friend that it would be indelicate to leave off stays. ...stays necessary for fashionable dress. p/c	
	3.7.1852 (478)	155	FLORENCE C: criticised by mother for giving up stays. p/c	

Vol.	Date	Page		
			press whilst supports it. The writer mentions "two London magazines supported chiefly by ladies.". p/c	He must mean *The Queen* and the *E.D.M.* He also condemns without giving its title: *The Corset and the Crinoline*.
	4.12.1869	508	SELINA P: indignant at previous points of letter quoted and Editor replies. p/c	
	12.2.1869	524	VIOLET INK and V.I.: quotes from two opposed to tight-lacing. p/c	
	8.1.1870	588	ANNIE MAY, M.S.C., ISABEL, A NON-SQUEEZER, A MOTHER: all support Editor against SELINA P. p/c	
	22.1.1870	620	ERISS and MINNIE: doubt that women should endanger their health, but they do. p/c	
	5.2.1870	652	ANNIE: advocates tight-lacing: looks best. Editor argues against. p/c	
	26.3.1870	764	BRIDGET ELIA: on folly of tight-lacing – has come across magazine which editor will not name [ie *E.D.M.*] p/c	
XLIV	12.1.1880 (supplement)		MADAM CARLSON's patent corsets, made by Herbert, Son, & Co., 73&74, Wood Street, E.C. p/c	
	21.2.1880	268	AUCKLAND: strong criticism of 'one of those perennial follies against which it is difficult to wage any new or novel argument'.	

for list of The Family Herald pages photocopied see Appendix One

6 *Chamber's Edinburgh Journal*

Vol.	Date	Page		
VI	15/8/1846	1024	"The use of the Corset", being a translation of a letter to a lady from Dr. Reveille-Parise.	Cited by Poole & Fletcher Strongly against tight-lacing

7 *Chamber's Miscellany of Useful and Entertaining Tracts*
(Edinburgh: William & Robert Chambers)

Vol.	Date	Page		
X	1846 (93)	8-16	VOLUNTARY DISTORTIONS – TIGHT-LACING	Illustrated with drawings of the bones of the chest etc. and quotations from medical writers: Samuel Hare, *Practical Observations on the Causes and Treatment of Curvature of the Spine* (London: Longman, 1838) William Coulson, *On Deformities of the Chest and Spine* (London: Longman, 1839), i.e. a revised and enlarged edition of the book mentioned at *3* above.

8 *Punch*

				Kunzle, ch. 3
11	1846	238	LECTURE ON TIGHT LACING: causes red noses, swollen ankles, etc.	K 137
43	20.9.1862	119	SUICIDE IN STAYS: tight lacing slow suicide: if smaller waist less likely to be married.	K 138
45	19.9.1863	122	FASHIONABLE SUICIDE	K 139
54	8.2.1868	64	A PLEA FOR TIGHT LACING: satirical comments on, and quotations from, The Englishwoman's Domestic Magazine.	K 140
57	18.9.1869	113	THE ELASTICITY OF YOUNG LADIES: satirical suggestion that Tight lacing harmful to men, but Not to women.	K 140
57	2.10.1869	126	A WANTON WARNING TO VANITY.	K 141

Vol.	Date	Page		
57	23.10.1869	162	THE TORMENTS OF TIGHT-LACING: spoof letter from A VICTIM hoping fashion will change.	K 140
57	20.11.1869	198	FASHIONABLE SUICIDE: another comment on the suicidal effect.	
58	7.5.1870	185	IS TIGHT-LACING INJURIOUS? spoof report of a ladies' debate on the subject.	K 140
59	24.9.1870	133	FAL-LALS AND FINE ART: spoof letter from NINA criticising the "frightful statues" of Greek art.	

9 Kidd's Own Journal

(started as *Kidd's London Journal* 3.1.1852, renamed 28.2.1852). *A Literary, Scientific, and Instructive Family Paper* edited by William Kidd of Hammersmith. (Monthly from January 1853, last number July 1854)

I	28.2.52	133-4	NATURE AND ART. A Comparison between Good Sense and "Fashion:" an attack on tight-lacing following a visit to Dr. Kahn's Anatomical Museum and quotations from Dr. L.J. Beale.	Dr Joseph Kahn was an Viennese doctor who ran a travelling museum, coming to England in 1851. The British Library has 4 editions of the catalogue of the exhibits, one of which was the wax figure of a woman of 18, whose attempt to conceal her pregnancy by continuing to tight lace, led to the death of both mother and child. Kahn's lectures and books on personal health are listed in the B.L. Catalogue. See Also *The Times*, 13.12. 1872, p.10e; 1.3.1873, p.11f and 19.12.1873, p.11e. The quotations are from *The Laws of Health* (1851).
II	7.8.52	88	Editorial comment on diminutive waists: "we … wonder what has become of their insides."	
III	Jan June 53	79-80	BAD HABITS, – THE USE AND ABUSE OF STAYS by W.H. Robertson, M.D.	
		160	WOMAN AND HER MAKER: Recommends the "Resilient Bodice" of Mesdames Maitland, 54, Connaught Terrace.	
IV	July 53-Jan 54	246	REFORM IN THE FEMALE FIGURE: the first reformers Mesdames Marion and Maitland, followed by Mesdames E. and E.H. Martin, 504, Oxford St. who have invented an elastic bodice to render stays unnecessary.	
		368	NATURE AND ART. A GENTLE HINT TO THE FAIR SEX: stays of Madame Caplin recommended: visit and interview.	
V	Feb-July 54	158	Review of *Elements of Health* by E.J. Tilt: "inestimable". Caplin's stays again recommended.	
		189	TIGHT LACING: JOHN C. claims one death from it.	
		244	THE FEMALE FIGURE: visit to, interview with, and description of corsets (*plastiques*) made by, Madame Vallotton at Madame Fontaine's, Jermyn St.	

10 Chamber's Journal
New Series

III	10.3.1855	153-5	ENGLAND AND THE ENGLISH by a Chinese. Includes a reference to young ladies "with pearl-white necks and tight-laced waists": "Nothing	Translation of a Chinese poem in the *North China Herald* about travels in England in 1844-5.

Vol.	Date	Page		

can possibly be so enchanting as to see ladies that compress themselves into taper forms of the most exquisite shape, the like of which I have never seen before."

11 *The Ladies' Treasury*

Founded April 1857

Vol.	Date	Page		
III	1.11.1859	346	THE USE AND MISUSE OF STAYS: Unsigned article critical of tight-lacing.	
VII	1.5.1863		TORTURE IN THE NINETEENTH CENTURY - FASHION IN TIGHT LACING: report of medical man: girls made to wear stays night and day.	Pages 11 and 14 of fashion supplement, immediately after p. 138.
VII	1.10.1863	298	TIGHT LACING: doctor rescues girl, fainting at dinner.	

12 *Once A Week*

Vol.	Date	Page		
VI	12.4.1862	445-6	STAYS: by John Plummer: Interesting article on the manufacture of stays. Statistics about extent and value of the manufacture of stays in Britain and about the import and export of stays – also quantity of materials used – number of people employed.	Cited in Poole & Fletcher. Passage of statistics quoted in *The Corset and The Crinoline* p195.

13 *The Queen*

Vol.	Date	Page		
	7.9.1861		Founded by S.O. Beeton. Frederick Greenwood appointed editor. Published at 248 Strand.	H. Montgomery Hyde: *Mr. & Mrs. Beeton*, (London, 1951) p121
	12.4.1862		Sold to Edward William Cox (proprietor of *The Field* and *The Law Times* etc.)	*The Queen* Centenary Issue, 3.8.1961, p150: see also D.N.B.: see also in general: Quentin Crewe, *The Frontiers of Privilege*. A century of social conflict as reflected in *The Queen* (London: Collins, 1961)
	12.4.1862 to 14.1.1865 inclusive		Printed and published by John Crockford at 346 Strand. see now my *Borrowed Plumes* (Liverpool: Karn Publications Garston, 1994) pp17-32	Statement at bottom right hand corner of last page of each issue. From an announcement in *The Field* 23.10.1858, p323, Crockford appears to have been the business manager of Cox's group of newspapers. 346 Strand was the address of these papers from 11.12.1858.
	12.4.1862	96	*The Queen* is edited by a lady. This has been elucidated by Charlotte C. Watkins in her, *Editing a 'Class Journal': Four Decades of The Queen* (Joel H. Weiner, ed. *Innovators and Preachers*, Westport, Connecticut: Greenwood Press, 1985) pp185-200. The editor was Helen Lowe from 1862 to 1894, when Percy Stuart Cox, son of Horace Cox, took over. I owe this reference to Kay Boardman.	It is not clear who this was or even whether it was true. Eliane de Marsy was the columnist on dress and fashions. By 2.1.1864 the statement had been modified to "This Department (i.e. 'Confidences') is Edited by a Lady; as are also the departments of 'Dress and Fashions', 'The Work-Table' and 'Domestic Economy'." The Queen was immediately remodelled on the lines of *The Field* with sections or departments on different subjects and correspondence and questions and answers about each subject. Prominence was given to 'Female Pastimes' and 'Womanly Exercises' with long instructional articles about Riding, Swimming, Croquet, Archery and Skating. There were also articles on women prominent in history under the title of 'Women who have appeared on the surface', the first of whom was the Chevalière d'Eon (18.4.1863) who, as a correspondent, H.G. (Paris) reminded the Editor on 17.10.1863 p261, was a man.

Vol.	Date	Page		
	14.7.1863		*The Queen* was merged with *The Lady's Newspaper*, and *The Court Chronicle*	The fifth volume of the paper is thus numbered vol. XXXIV. I can find no trace of *The Court Chronicle*.
	21.1.1865		Printed and Published for the proprietors by John Pownall Chorley	Chorley was publisher of *The Field* (bottom right hand corner of last page)
	28.1.1865		ditto By Horace Cox	nephew of Edward William Cox became editor according to *The Queen* Centenary Issue p150 (but see previous page).

Correspondence, articles etc. about corsets and tight-lacing are as follows:

Vol.	Date	Page		
II	26.4.1862	141	ADVERT by W. Carter, 22 Ludgate Street for 'Sylphide' corset – an "anti-consumptive elastic corset".	
	28.6.1862	330	A FATHER: asks for a work on the evils of tight-lacing "as practised to such an extent by the young ladies of the present day?"	The Editor knows of none – invites readers to give the information.
	5.7.1862	351	TIGHT-LACING: William Kidd cites, *'Elements of Health'* by E.J.Tilt.	Edward John Tilt, *Elements of Health and Principles of Female Hygiene* (London: Bohn, Covent Garden, 1852)
	12.7.1862	372	D.G.S.: cites *Chambers Miscellany of Useful and Entertaining Tracts*, vol X, seventh article: *'Voluntary Distortions: tight-lacing'* from W. & R. Chambers, Edinburgh. A FATHER: thanks Mr. Kidd	see *6*
	9.8.1862	448	LADIES FIGURES: Frank Buckland cites the example of Brahmin girls carrying water pots.	Francis Trevelyn Buckland 1826-1880 contributor to *The Field* from 1856, started own paper *Land & Water* 1866. Doctor and naturalist. See George C. Bompas, *Life of Frank Buckland* (London: Nelson, 1885) and G.H.O. Burgess, *The Curious World of Frank Buckland*, (London: 1967)
	23.8.1862	492	LADIES FIGURES: FIREFLY: thinks Brahmin girls benefit from absence of restraint on their bodies; commends Welsh country girls.	The nom-de-plume 'Firefly' appears in *The Field* from 1857. Regular contributor to *F.* and *Q.*
III	6.9.1862	11	LADIES FIGURES: further brief comment by Frank Buckland.	
	6.12.1862	250	KNITTED STAYS: Two correspondents give information.	
XXXIV	18.7.1863	44	THE CORSET – THE SLENDER WAIST: CONSTANCE: is it true becoming fashionable? claims to be 16½".	Reproduced in *The Corset and The Crinoline* p155
	25.7.1863	55	FANNY: fashionable? YES: went to Parisian school.	*The Corset and The Crinoline* p156
	1.8.1863	80	Frank Buckland: Against A COUNTRY SUBSCRIBER: strong attack on CONSTANCE ELIZA: In favour; her own waist 16" G.C.C.: long letter against: proportion; she is 23½" over her dress, 5' 5¾" in her boots.	*The Corset and The Crinoline* p159
	8.8.1863	99	CORSETS AND SLENDER WAISTS: NATURA: doubts 16½"	

Vol.	Date	Page		
			FIREFLY: against	Firefly was a regular lady contributor who had also written for *The Field*.
			LE COMTE DE MANIN: against	
			ADMIRER: tries to refute the anti-corset party.	*The Corset and The Crinoline* p160 In opinion and in some phrases very similar to *The Corset Defended* by Madame de la Santé.
	15.8.1863	115	SLENDER WAISTS AND CORSETS: VNA: against	
			Frank Buckland: cites *The Penny Magazine* 28.2.1833. Also dressed a Greek statue in modern dress.	Quoted in *The Corset Defended*, p14 and *The Corset and The Crinoline* p180: see **2**
	22.8.1863	128	*'Mr. Surly Hardrake on Tight-lacing'* – a satirical article by J.J.B.	Apparently John James Britton by whom there are a novel and 2 or 3 volumes of poems in British Library Catalogue. He was a regular contributor.
	5.12.1863	375	HISTORY OF THE CORSET: unsigned article.	Largely based on Strutt and used by author of *The Corset Defended*.
		376	THE CORSET QUESTION: ELIZA K: regrets no more letters.	
	19.12.1863	411	CORSETS AND SMALL WAISTS: ELIZA K: praises the article on history of corset.	
XXXV	20.2.1864	145	CORSETS AND SMALL WAISTS: A FORMER CORRESPONDENT (Edinburgh) wants more letters; tiny waists in portraits; daughters corseted from 7.	*The Corset and The Crinoline* p165 *Figure Training* p32 This writer is possibly ADMIRER (8.8.1863) and also MADAME DE LA SANTÉ
	5.3.1864	193	CORSETS AND SLENDER WAISTS: A FORMER CORRESPONDENT (Edinburgh) gives further description of her methods.	
	12.3.1864	213	CORSETS AND SMALL WAISTS: WHALEBONE: says came in during reign of Henry II of France	
	19.3.1864	233	CORSETS AND SMALL WAISTS A FORMER CORRESPONDENT: makes a correction	
XXXVI	27.8.1864	129	STAYS: two French makers recommended; Madame Fay, 18 Baker Street, Madame Laroache, 10 Sale Street, Cambridge Terrace, Edgware Road.	
XXXVI	25.2.1865	127	*The Corset Defended*	Review – see **14** (and Appendix Two)
	17.6.1865	400	A COUNTRY READER: should a riding-belt or stays be worn on horseback?	
	24.6.1865	416	GRACE, KATE, FILLE DE L'AIR and MINA F: all say stays. The latter recommends Mrs. Stirling Clarke, *The Habit and the Horse*.	
XXXIX	23.6.1866	483	WHALEBONE STAYS: A WIDOWER: should the female body be encased in whale bone stays? Daughter complains of her finishing school.	
	30.6.1866	502	ZOPETA: wants to know what A WIDOWER's daughter's training is?	
XL1	2.5.1868		*The Corset and the Crinoline*	Favourable review: see Kunzle pp. 222 and 251.

Vol.	Date	Page		

14 The Englishwomans' Domestic Magazine

	May 1852		Founded by S.O. Beeton (born 2.3.1831)	*'Cupid's Letter Bag'* from May 1852 replaced by *'The Conversazione'* from May 1860 – normally answers to correspondents on dress making, household management and etiquette. Also some letters selected for comment.
			Published in 3 series May 1852 – Apr 1860 May 1860 – Dec 1864 Jan 1865 – 1879	
	10.7.1856		Married Isabella Mayson.	
	6.2.1865		Isabella died.	
	1866		Beeton in financial trouble, works under Ward, Lock and Tyler.	
	Jan 1867		Magazine refashioned.	Enlarged 'Conversazione' from Jan 1867 with long letters published in full.
	6.6.1877		Beeton died.	

Material on Corsets and Tight-lacing is as follows:

V	July 1862	144	SERAPHINE: writes to ask 'what is the smallest size waist known' – claims to be 15¾" – recommended not to tight lace.	This letter was not reproduced. It was merely used for comment.
VIII	November 1863	48	A VICTIM: writes to us – eight closely-written pages – on a subject of very serious importance, that of having her poor ribs tortured into a fashionable figure.	
VIII	April 1864	288	LUCY: why shouldn't your brother wear stays?	Kunzle, p 251, n.10
II	Sept. 1866	272	Article in the Series *'The Human Form Divine'* on *'The Waist'*	Tinted plate with article on opposite page.
III	March 1867	164-5	A LADY FROM EDINBURGH: invites correspondence – daughter subjected to 'merciless system of tight lacing.'	*The Corset and The Crinoline* p172
	April 1867	223-4	STAYLACE: thinks previous letter 'made up for a purpose' – 'To me the sensation of being tightly laced in a pair of elegant, well made. tightly fitting corsets is superb...'.	*The Corset and The Crinoline* p173
	May 1867	276	BELLE: approves of STAYLACE	*The Corset and The Crinoline* p175
			MEDICUS: moderate compression not injurious.	*The Corset and The Crinoline* p154 *Figure Training* p45
			H.W.: advice given to ladies about a waistband.	
		277	X.Y.Z.: recommends THE THOMSON CORSET.	
		279	NORA: was at school where girls tightly-laced – no ill effects.	*The Corset and The Crinoline* p170, *Figure Training* p83. Also reproduced by Norah Waugh *Corsets and Crinolines* (London: B.T. Batsford, 1954) p141
			A CONSTANT SUBSCRIBER: reassures mother of tight-laced girl – knows a girl 13" at 17 now 22" at 27, recovered by lying down a little each day.	
	June 1867	333-4	THE YOUNG LADY HERSELF: confirms her mother's letter (March 1867)	*The Corset and The Crinoline* p176
		334	BRISBANE: against tight-lacing.	
		335	A SCHOOLMISTRESS CORRESPONDENT: defends the fashion.	*The Corset and The Crinoline* p177

Vol.	Date	Page		

Vol.	Date	Page		
		112	A COLONEL: proposed figure-training for daughter – to have backboard.	*Figure Training* p56
			M.C.: recommends A WIDOWER to have daughters' figures trained. Son fitted with stays when seven, still wears now married. Many men wear belts – 9 to 20 inches in depth. Has made stays for gentlemen.	*Figure Training* p100
			AN IRISHWOMAN: astonished that the letters on tight-lacing are genuine. Won't believe any written by men. 'And I will believe that the writers represent the most silly of my sex, and hope they belong to a very small minority, *getting still smaller.*' (This seems certain. Ed)	
	Sept. 1868	165-6	E.R.: delighted with *The Corset and The Crinoline* mentions reviews in *Spectator* and *Saturday Review*.	
		166	LA GÈNE: a widower, agrees about tight-lacing for girls. Although does not wear stays himself ('rather a disgusting idea').	
			F.C and A.L.: Both men ask how to get – want to try.	
		167	GOWNSMAN: admires tight-lacing.	
	October 1868	224	ANOTHER WIDOWER: wants staymaker for stays and backboards for daughter (apply to Madame Delagarde, Cranbourne Street, Leicester Square.)	
			JERRY: has worn leather chest-expanding braces under dress – good for growing girls and boys 14 to 18. She has known many gentlemen wear them.	
			ENQUIRER: seeks information about method of lacing from PERSEVERANCE.	
			H.G.: a man, got corsets from Miss P. Lowry, 3 Featherstone Buildings, High Holborn – experimented for 6 weeks delighted with and continued wearing.	
	Nov. 1868	277	MINNIE BELL: against tight-lacing, thoroughly disgusted by men who do it.	
			BADEN-BADEN: tight-lacing not in favour in Paris.	
			H.T.: comments on the illustrations in *The Corset and The Crinoline*.	
			R.W.: a married man, has worn ladies' stays for 3 or 4 years, very comfortable indeed, recommends Mrs. Shute's, 9 Tottenham Court Road.	
			AURA ANTILACE: opposed to tight-lacing has 28" waist.	
	December 1868	314	SILKWORM: mentions *'Line of Beauty'* Corset by Johnson, Hatchman & Co. pp325-6	
		327	LUCINA: against tight-lacing.	

Vol.	Date	Page		
	April 1871	254-5	EMILY D: never worn stays until married at 20. Height 5' 3", waist 26" now 18" in corset. Has persuaded husband to wear a corset for a weakness in his back (a bank clerk).	

256 WILLIAM S'ARRAC: explains to A STAID MAN why corset-wearing men persecuted. A danger of a flood of effeminacy immersing the Anglo-Saxon race. Such men tend to lower men in the estimation of women; throw themselves open to attack by Miss Becker and other violent women. The fair sex will assume all men to be despised.

June 1871   380   F. BROOKE: letters on tight-lacing are distasteful to the 'more sensible and intellectual subscribers'.

M.B.: very pleased with letters from WILLIAM S'ARRAC criticises EMILY D. – why reduce her husband's waist? He is 5' 5", waist 22", age 20. When younger tried his sister's stays for 3 days but no longer. Pain in back disgusted him with wasp-waist.

XI   July 1871   61   L'AMI: mentions *The Art of Figure Training* – approves.   *The Art of Figure Training* published May 1871

M.A. (CAMBRIDGE) discusses *Figure Training* disagrees with AN OLD STAY-WEARER on 2 points. He prefers front lacing and leather stays, describes how to make. William S'Arrac views absurd. Military men have always cultivated figures.   *Figure Training* p51

62 ENDURANCE: describes ways of locking stays behind.

August 1871   126   NICE LOOKING BUT NOT PRETTY: about fact that Englishwomen not well dressed ...need to have well designed fitted corsets ...'Even the chemise of a Parisian is shaped with due regard to her figure, and folds of longcloth or cambric are *not* squeezed under tight corsets. The same care is bestowed on the camisole, the jupon, the tournure or crinoline' ...merits of French dress makers.

127 PERSEVERANCE: about good carriage and upright figure ...quotes from Heather Bigg: *Manual of Orthopraxy* 1869, where disuse of backboard regretted, also from *Edinburgh Review* October 1869 about training of Miss Edgeworth with backboards, etc. ...has tried in vain to obtain a backboard ...describes method of making a brace for attachment to the stays.   I could not find this in the *Edinburgh Review* of October 1869 (vol. 130)

E.S.: *Gentlemen's Corsets* necessary to have stiff stays laced up tight in the morning for reduction of size – thinks men's stays should lace in front – suggests shop with male attendants – laces for health and pleasure but not all day.

Sept. 1871   191   E.M.: mentions a former letter reprinted in *Art of Figure Training*, discusses an improvement on the Austrian shoulder straps ...'They rather

HUMMING-BIRD is the new fashion editor from January 1875.

15 The Corset Defended

by Madame de la Santé
Published by T. E. Carler: London. 1865
Printed by Robert K. Burt, Holborn Hill.
Price eighteen pence

This is a pamphlet of 31 pages. It was received in the British Museum on the 30th January 1865 and is bound up with other *Tracts 1852-74*, all about costume, at shelf-mark 7743.b.56(5). The pseudonym appears not to have been identified but I feel fairly confident that the authoress is the lady who wrote letters to *The Queen* under the nom de plume ADMIRER (8.8.1863 – see *The Corset and The Crinoline* p160) and A FORMER CORRESPONDENT (Edinburgh) (20.2.1864 – see *The Corset and The Crinoline* p165, 5.3.1864 and 19.3.1864). There are overwhelming similarities of style and content. She also quotes from a letter from Frank Buckland of 15.8.1863, which was in part a reply to the letter from ADMIRER. She was therefore certainly familiar with the correspondence in *The Queen* and may have decided to amplify her views in the form of a pamphlet. By the time it appeared, the correspondence in *The Queen* on the subject of the corset had come to an end, but there is a review of it on 25.2.1865 (see Appendix 2). It is quoted from with the author and title given by a correspondent in *The Young Englishwoman* on 14.10.1865. Thereafter author and title are not referred to together in any Beeton or Ward, Lock publication. Perhaps Beeton had begun to think of using it in connection with a publication of his own. TRY IT refers to *The Corset Defended* without mentioning the author in the *E.D.M.* of March 1869, but it is significant that in the reprinting of this letter in *Figure Training* (see below) p49, this title is omitted. VERNON is also allowed to mention an alleged second edition of *The Corset Defended* in the *E.D.M.* of February 1871.

It is the first of four booklets about corsets and tight-lacing which appeared between 1865 and 1871. Although the writer is in favour of the corset, she is the least extreme and in fact condemns tight-lacing. Unfortunately her little pamphlet appears to have been largely forgotten, probably because it was swallowed up and swamped by *The Corset and The Crinoline*.

Contents:

Chapter I	The Origin and History of the Corset	The chapter headings give a sufficient idea of her thesis. The Corset has a long history.
Chapter II	The Waist of Nature or the Waist of Art	Other nations and societies have admired the small waist and have suffered to achieve it.
Chapter III	The Present Fashion	The present fashion is both moderate and elegant.
Chapter IV	The Corset Unjustly Condemned	Criticism of the corset is based on the very stiff straight stays of the 18th century, it is now out of date and inapplicable to the modern corset. Much of the medical opinion is erroneous and misconceived.
Chapter V	Its Proper Construction	The corset should be firmly made, not of elastic. It should have a front fastening busk with shoulder straps for growing girls. When it is being fitted, the hips and chest should be measured as well as the waist and the corsets should meet when laced on.
Chapter VI	How to secure a Slender Figure without Compression	Training for the corset should begin at the age of seven or eight and should proceed by gradual stages. There should be no need to resort to 'tight-lacing'. The authoress condemns the use of corsets by night which she claims both to have come across herself (see quotation in *The Corset and The Crinoline* p153) and to have read about in 'the public journals' within the last three or four years.

16 *The Young Englishwoman*

Vol.	Date	Page		
	31.2.1864		weekly, founded by S. O. Beeton monthly from 1867.	
II	14.10.1865	256	THE CORSET: A correspondent (Manchester) sends a quotation from *The Corset Defended* by Madame de la Santé about corset training and lacing of girls 7 to 8.	*The Corset Defended* published 30.1.1865. This is the only full mention of title and author in the Beeton publications.
I N.S.	May 1867	277	Correspondents on corsets invited to write to *E.D.M.*	Evidence of a deliberate policy to make *E.D.M.* a vehicle for this.
II N.S.	May 1868	277	FOURTEEN INCHES: comments on the tight-lacing controversy.	
	November 1868	616	recommends *Line of Beauty* corsets made by Johnson, Hatchman & Co. of 3&4 Little Love Lane.	

Vol.	Date	Page		
	December 1868	664	ROBIN ADAIR: Apply to Johnson Hatchman & Co., of 3&4 Little Love Lane, Wood Street, Cheapside.	Could be same writer who wrote to *E.D.M.* September 1870 and several times thereafter.
	January 1875		SYLVIA took over from MYRA as editress. MYRA started *Myra's Journal of Dress and Fashion* at the same time.	
	January 1878		Continued as *Sylvia's Home Journal*.	
	May 1878	235	SMALL WAIST: man cites correspondence in *The Englishwoman's Domestic Magazine*: has worn stays ever since. Are stays for men on increase?	
	July 1878	293	SYLVIA'S LETTER: opposed to tight-lacing: Quotes Mrs. Haweis [*The Art of Beauty* (1878) or *The Art of Dress* (1879)].	
	Sept. 1878	419	MARGARET'S SISTER: thanks SYLVIA for previous comment: long letter on the serious folly of tight-lacing: has given up stays: now wears flannel bodice.	Steele 166
	Jan. 1879	10	SARAH JANE: agrees on tight-lacing.	
	July 1879	256	HARRY: replies to SMALL WAIST: wears stays, has weak spine. Also thinks ladies' dress "is quite as healthy and decidedly more comfortable to wear, than the unromantic, ugly costume we are compelled to don."	This is an early preference for female attire. See my *Men in Petticoats*.
	Oct. 1879	364	THOMAS: agrees with HARRY: not ridiculous to wear stays for support: he does so in rural life. Where obtain? (This closes the correspondence on a subject of very little interest to ladies, for whom the Journal is specially intended.)	

17 The Young Ladies' Journal
[started 13.4.1864]

Vol.	Date	Page		
III	1.10.1866	591	MABEL VAUGHAN: advised small waists not in fashion.	K. 251, n. 11: I could not find "misguided reader" mentioned by K.
	1.12.1866	783	LACEE: editor supports her complaint against her mother subjecting her to tight-lacing.	
	1.1.1867	846	A FEW WORDS ON TIGHT LACING by a physician.	
IV	1.2.1867	14	ON THE EVILS OF TIGHT LACING: continuation of article with diagrams.	

18 The Corset and The Crinoline

by W.B.L.
Ward, Lock & Tyler: London, 1868
British Library Catalogue 7742.b.36

This work is partly an illustrated review of the whole history of Women's costume and partly a selection of letters from *The Queen* and *E.D.M.*

The forthcoming production of this book was announced in the *E.D.M.* of November 1867. It is curious however that the writer speaks of a letter to *The Queen* in the issue of 20.2.1864 as having appeared *'a few months ago'* which suggests that the work was in contemplation somewhat earlier than the correspondence in the *E.D.M.* started. Perhaps it was started in 1865 after the publication of *The Corset Defended* to which it owes so much.
The Corset and The Crinoline was announced as ready in the *E.D.M.* of May 1868. It was reviewed by *The Saturday Review* of 23.5.1868, *London Society*, October 1869 and *The Family Herald*, 31.10.1869. According to the *Dictionary of*

Anonymous and Pseudonymous English Literature, vol. I, p437 the initials W.B.L. stand for William Barry Lord. I have not been able to find out anything about him but the *Dictionary* cites two later works by Lord:

1) *The Key to Fortune in New Lands; and handbook of the 'Explorers' Test Case'* by W.B.L. London: 1869 (vol III, p216)

2) *Diamonds and Gold: the three main routes to the South African Ophir, and how to equip for the journey*, by W.B.L. ppii. 95 London: 1871 (vol II p57).

Perhaps Lord went abroad after the publication of *The Corset and The Crinoline*.

Contents:

Chapter I	The Use of The Corset among Savage Tribes and Ancient Peoples	Several of Madame de la Santé's references used plus new material and quotations from Fullom's History of Woman (Stephen Watson Fullom, *The History of Woman, and her Connexion with religion, civilization and domestic manners, from the earliest period*, 2 vols. London: 1855. There were 3 editions in 1855. Published novels and general literature 1851-71; not in DNB), and from Sir Gardner Wilkinson's *Manners and Customs of The Ancient Egyptians*, London: 1837-41
Chapter II	Classical Times	Largely based on Strutt's Introduction to his *Dress and Habits of the people of England* (1796-1799), together with one or two passages derived from Santé and quotations from Fullom.
Chapter III	Early Middle Ages in France	Nearly all Strutt with some help from Santé.
Chapter IV	Renaissance in France and England	Quotations from Philip Stubs taken from Strutt; also one or two hints from Santé.
Chapter V	17th Century France and England	Some quotations from Strutt.
Chapter VI	18th Century	Several letters from *The Guardian* of 1713, – a source indicated by Santé.
Chapter VII	Late 18th and Early 19th	Relies heavily on Santé: then the quotations from *The Queen & E.D.M.* begin.
Chapters VIII to X	Mainly letters from *The Queen & E.D.M.* In chapter X details are also given of *Thomson's* glove fitting corsets and of the *Redresseur* corset of Vienna.	In chapters V to VII Lord may have also used the various pamphletts which were produced by makers of crinolines. I have found the following references to these:

1) Edward Philpott: *History of Crinoline: An historical account of the Farthingale and Hoop petticoat*, London, 1863 (extracts and illustrations from in *The Queen* 16.5.1863)

2) Advertisement by Edward Philpott, *Family Draper and Jupon Manufacturer, 37, Piccadilly* for *Illustrated Pamphlett on Crinolines, from 1559 to 1863*, post free.(*The Queen* 2.1.1864 p31)

3) Edward Philpott: *Crinolines in our parks and promenades from 1730 to 1864 with antique illustrations*: 1864. (Article about this with 2 illustrations, *The Queen* 21.5.1864 pp404-5)

4) The above may be the work cited in the

British Library Catalogue as:
Edward Philpott: *Crinoline from 1730 to 1864*
London 1864 (1754.a.17). Doris Langley
Moore quotes from this in her *The Woman in Fashion* (London: 1949) p70.

5) *A few Observations on Crinolines* issued free by post by Addley Bourne, Family Draper, Jupon and Corset Manufacturer to the Court and Royal Family, 37, Piccadilly (A passage was quoted from this in *The Young Englishwoman* 9.6.1865, p384. The address is the same as for (2) above and all may in fact be versions of the same thing.

After further study of these pamphlets I do not think Lord used them. Philpott was a manufacturer of crinolines himself and his booklets were part of the publicity for his products. In (4) for example he advertised his own *Sanflectum Crinolines*. *The Corset and The Crinoline*, however, advertised Thomson's corsets and his *Zephyrina* crinolines and Thomson must have sponsored or paid for this advertising in some way.

On the other hand, another little booklet I purchased recently, The First and Second Empire of Crinoline (26 pages, no date or publisher, coloured plates front and back) was certainly based on *The Corset and The Crinoline*. The covers mentioned and nearly all the engravings inside are taken from *The Corset and The Crinoline*. The front cover is a coloured version of *Crinoline in 1713* on page 114. Also at the end of the booklet are several pages advertising Thomson's crinolines and corsets. On the last two pages is a poem extolling the virtues of the crinoline and in particular the *Zephyrina*. no doubt Thomson produced this little booklet for his own purposes.

About 30 passages in *The Corset and The Crinoline* can be traced to Santé's booklet and a larger quantity to Strutt. In neither case does Lord mention the name of the relevant work. Although occasionally passages occur in quotation marks, quite often large chunks are taken from Strutt and smaller pieces from Santé without any indication of the source. Often Strutt's words are reproduced exactly while Santé's are rephrased. He mentions Santé four times and here he does put her actual words in quotation marks.

The letters from The Queen and E.D.M. reproduced in *The Corset and The Crinoline* are listed in Appendix Three

Six letters from *The Queen* and twenty-two from the *E.D.M.* are included, not in chronological order but to suit the author's argument.

It is highly significant that none of the letters opposing tight-lacing are reproduced.

The work is thus not only derivative but thoroughly biassed. It is unreliable both as History and as a guide to contemporary opinion.

19 The Saturday Review

25   23.5.1868   695-6   Review of *The Corset and The Crinoline*.

A highly critical Review:
"*The Corset and The Crinoline* is a daring book. It is written to show that the greatest aim of feminine fashions at all times has been the creation of a small waist, and to advocate the continuance of that aim. We thought we had done with this senseless barbarism, whatever else might remain, and that, though fat girls and portly matrons do undoubtedly need some support and perhaps a little gentle compression, the craze for a wasp's waist caused by steel and whalebone had died out, and that we were too far advanced on the way of true civilisation in dress to bring it to life again. ... We are sorry to see so silly and, we must add, so mischievious a book as this *Corset and The Crinoline* in print."

It is interesting, however, that the reviewer does not challenge the veracity of any of the correspondents quoted in *The Corset and The Crinoline*.

The Corset and The Crinoline was also strongly criticised by Mrs E. Lynn Linton in her essay *The Follies of Fashion* (*Ourselves: Essays on Women*: London 1869, New Edition 1884 pp157-160)

20 The Spectator

23.5.1868   610-12   STAYS: long condemnatory review of *The Corset and the Crinoline*, quoting extracts.

Kunzle 226: contrary to what Kunzle says, the title is given.

21 The Tomahawk

4.7.1868   8   *The Corset and the Crinoline*: brief review: contemptible subject, recommended to no one.

K 225-6 and 251

22 London Society

October 1869   312-19   *Corsets and Corpulence*. Review of *The Corset and The Crinoline*.

The reviewer gives a good summary of the book, and although he expresses some reservations about the credibility of the statements made in it, he defends the use of the corset and moderately tight-lacing in general. He cannot believe that it can be so harmful as its opponents make out, since it has been persisted in so long. 'They cannot all be so foolish as to mistake pain for pleasure and bad health for good.' The review includes a letter from a man who describes his success in using leather corsets to reduce corpulence.

23 The Freaks of Fashion

With illustrations of the changes in the corset and the crinoline, from remote periods to the present time. ppxii, 227
Ward, Lock & Tyler: 1870.

The British Library Catalogue (7742.bb.64) notes the entry in brackets 'A reissue of *The Corset and The Crinoline*' and apart from the title page, it is exactly the same as the first edition of that book.
This title is never referred to in *E.D.M.* or in other of Beeton's magazines.

24 Madre Natura versus The Moloch of Fashion

A Social Essay, with Thirty Illustrations by Luke Limner
Chatto & Windus: London, 1870
Fourth Edition 1874

Luke Limner was the pen-name of John Leighton (1822-1912), an artist, one of the original proprietors of *The Graphic* (*Who was Who 1897-1916*: London, 1920).

This book is an amusing but long-winded attack on fashion in general and on the corset in particular. The author brings into action again the 18th century physicians denounced by Madame de la Santé and gives a long list of the diseases caused by tight-lacing. Some of his illustrations are comic but he gives the usual diagrams of the female internal organs before and after tight-lacing. He may have copied these from a medical source but the diagrams in Joseph Farrar's *Lung Capacity and tight-lacing* (*Good Words*, vol 21: 1880 pp202-205) are very similar – except for the heads. Ada S. Ballin prints similar diagrams in her *Science of Dress* (1885).

The fact that the book went into four editions by 1874 indicates the popularity of his point of view.

25 General Sir Ian Hamilton: When I Was a Boy

Faber & Faber: London, 1939
Speaking of his summer holidays in Scotland in 1870, the author writes: 'On week-days I had my boat, which had cost £25, and there were the Alexander Dennistouns at Roselea, a pretty place on the Point which jutted out between the Goreloch and Loch Long. There many roses grew – including a bunch of pretty daughters: Edith, Augusta, Kathy and Beryl, all tall and fit and supple(!) although they had the smallest waists in Scotland, Kathy's being 14 inches and the others' 15 inches. The sun-basking damsels of today may raise those streaks of pencil they call eyebrows, but not only was I told this over and over again, but I have squared these circles myself and so should know. We were very correct young people, though, and a strict etiquette cut out any joke with the remotest tinge of impropriety or vulgarity' (p191-192).

Although written by a very old man, this reminiscence carries conviction and gives a very interesting instance of tight-lacing claims by named individuals and the circumstances in which they were made. If Hamilton measured their waists as he seems to be claiming, it may of course be doubted how exact or accurate his measuring was.

26 Figure Training; or Art The Handmaid of Nature

by E.D.M. p125
Ward, Lock & Tyler: London (no date)
The first chapter repeats much of what had already been argued in *The Corset and The Crinoline* often in the same words and using the same quotations.

British Library (7743.b.44). This copy bears the date 26 May 1871.

This work was not apparently by W.B. Lord as the initials W.B.L. would presumably have been used again. In any case, as suggested above, Lord may have been abroad after 1868, engaged partly at least in writing other books.

As already seen, the editor of *E.D.M.* had invited contributions to another work on figure training in October 1870.

The letters quoted either wholly or in part are listed in Appendix Four (there are some new letters).

Several had previously appeared in *The Corset and The Crinoline* (as noted in Appendix Four). As in the case of *The Corset and The Crinoline* no letters critical of tight-lacing are included.

27 Charles Reade: A Simpleton, A Story of the Day.

3 vols. (London: Chapman & Hall, 1873).
Husband contends with tight-Lacing wife.

Kunzle 130-2
Steele 169

THE FAMILY HERALD
(founded 13 May 1843)

List of pages photocopied:	*Answers to Correspondents and Articles on Stays and Tight-lacing.*
29 April 1848	LILY
13 May 1848	MASSY MAGPIE
3 June 1848	CANARY BIRD
17 June 1848	ISABELLA G.
24 June 1848	ROSY CHEEK HERMINIE SNAILIOLA
26 August 1848	AUGUSTA M.
11 November 1848	Tight Lacing
23 December 1848	LOCASTRIA
20 January 1849	GEORGINA C.
17 February 1849	JANE ANNE
3 March 1849	MARIANNE F.
12 May 1849	GEORGIANA
15 December 1849	ELLEN R.
12 June 1852	LOLA A.
3 July 1852	FLORENCE C.
8 January 1853	MARIE H.
7 January 1854	Stays
1 March 1856	A Few Hints on Stays
30 August 1856	The Construction of Corsets etc.
22 November 1856	Stays and Bodies
27 December 1856	The Art of Making Stays etc.
7 February 1857	Madame Caplin's Corsets
9 March 1861	ANTI-CORSET
27 June 1863	SERRÉS PAR UN LACET
29 August 1863	ÉLÉGANTE
3 October 1863	BLACK POLE
21 November 1863	A LONDON LADY-PRINCIPAL
18 January 1864	FAIRPLAY
30 October 1869	Tight Lacing and Wasp Waists (review of *The Corset and The Crinoline*)
4 December 1869	SELINA P.
11 December 1869	VIOLET INK and V.I.
8 January 1870	ANNIE MAY, M.S.C., ISABEL, A NON-SQUEEZER and A MOTHER
22 January 1870	ERISS and MINNIE
5 February 1870	ANNIE
26 March 1870	BRIDGET ELIA
12 January 1880	Madame Carlson's Corsets

Review of The Corset Defended in The Queen
(25 February 1865 p127)

Our readers cannot fail to remember the animated discussion which took place in our columns some months ago on the subject of tight-lacing. The authoress of the pamphlet before us was one of the many who joined heartily in the debate, and on several occasions propounded her theories on this corset question. Like all other questions, every possible shade of opinion is held on it, from that which advocates tight-lacing down to that which counsels the wearing of no stays at all. And, after all that can be said for and against the adoption of corsets, and the exact degree to which they should be laced, we think that the generality of sensible women have come to the conclusion that if well cut, slightly stiffened, and laced evenly without pressure, corsets can be worn with advantage as well as comfort by every well-grown, well-developed figure. As to the exact dimensions of what a waist *ought* to measure, that is an unanswerable question, as so much depends on height, and also on the width of the shoulders. A narrow-chested young lady, with a seventeen-inch waist, may look anything but shapely, while a twenty-two-inch waist, with a broad chest and shoulders, will, on the contrary, appear slender. Proportion and roundness are the main points to be considered in judging of a good figure; all sudden curves are incompatible with lines of beauty.

There is no doubt but that it is the fashion of the day to admire slender waists; and if this desired object can be obtained without compression or any other hurtful measure, so much the better. The following is the plan which our authoress recommends after, she informs us, "several years' experience in the education of girls," and which she has found to be attended with unvarying success: "At the age of seven or eight years, girls should be carefully measured and fitted with stays, made so as to meet from top to bottom, when laced on. When so laced there should be no tightness whatever round the chest or below the waist, and they should be little more than close-fitting even at the waist itself. These corsets should be furnished with shoulder-straps, which should not be felt when the shoulders are held in their proper position. The chest and hip gores should be made to lace, so as to permit of their being let out gradually as the girls grow, thus avoiding any pressure whatever on those parts. The shoulder-straps will likewise require a small alteration occasionally. When new stays are necessary, they should be made to the same pattern and to *the same waist measure*, but as much larger in other respects as the former pair had become by being let out, and, of course, a little longer. By this simple and rational method the figure will be *directed* instead of *forced* into a slender shape." Having never seen this plan tried we cannot speak to its efficacy, but we had hitherto considered corsets unnecessary until a girl had attained to ten or even to twelve years of age, and that then they should be of the lightest and softest make. But with the authoress we perfectly coincide in her opinion that corsets should be *well* made, and properly fitted to individual figures. The 'ready-made' are very convenient for those who are slight naturally, but for those who have any pretensions to a well developed figure the trifling additional expense of being fitted by a skilful maker will be amply repaid by the results. The pamphlet contains many interesting details of the origin and history of the corset.

[I owe this reference to Valerie Steele.]

LETTERS IN THE CORSET AND THE CRINOLINE
Letters from The Queen and E.D.M. are as follows:

Publication	Date	Page	Correspondent	
E.D.M.	November 1867	136	WALTER	a male stay-wearer
E.D.M.	October 1867	149	MIGNONETTE	
E.D.M.	November 1867	150	DEBUTANTE	
E.D.M.	May 1867	154	MEDICUS	
The Queen	18 July 1863	155	CONSTANCE	
The Queen	25 July 1863	156	FANNY	
The Queen	1 August 1863	159	ELIZA	
The Queen	8 August 1863	160	ADMIRER	} probably Madame de la Santé
The Queen	20 February 1864	165	A FORMER CORRESPONDENT	
E.D.M.	January 1868	168	A TIGHT-LACER	
E.D.M.	January 1868	169	JEZEBEL	
E.D.M.	May 1867	170	NORA	also reproduced by Norah Waugh *Corsets and Crinolines* p141
E.D.M.	March 1867	172	A LADY FROM EDINBURGH	This is the first letter in the series.
E.D.M.	April 1867	173	STAYLACE	
E.D.M.	May 1867	175	BELLE	
E.D.M.	June 1867	176	THE YOUNG LADY HERSELF	
E.D.M.	June 1867	177	A SCHOOLMISTRESS CORRESPONDENT	
E.D.M.	February 1868	179	MIGNON	
The Queen	15 August 1863	180	FRANK BUCKLAND	part only
E.D.M.	September 1867	180	ANOTHER ARTIST	
E.D.M.	September 1867	181	ANOTHER CORRESPONDENT	
E.D.M.	September 1867	182	AN INVETERATE TIGHT-LACER	
E.D.M.	October 1867	184	A YOUNG BARONET	
E.D.M.	November 1867	184	BENEDICT	
E.D.M.	November 1867	192	EDINA	
E.D.M.	July 1867	214	EFFIE MARGETSON	
E.D.M.	July 1867	214	L. THOMPSON	
E.D.M.	September 1867	215	AN OLD SUBSCRIBER	

LETTERS IN FIGURE TRAINING; OR ART THE HANDMAID OF NATURE

Publication	Date	Page	Correspondent	
unnamed paper	1842	25		also in *The Corset and The Crinoline* p194 in which the paper was described as a 'very talented and well-conducted journal'.
The Queen	20.2.1864	32	A FORMER CORRESPONDENT	*The Corset and The Crinoline* p165
		39	A.F. M.D.	a special letter to the Compiler of the book
E.D.M.	January 1871	43	S.	a male stay-wearer
E.D.M.	May 1867	45	MEDICUS	*The Corset and The Crinoline* p 154
E.D.M.	September 1867	46	AN INVETERATE TIGHT-LACER	*The Corset and The Crinoline* p 182
E.D.M.	May 1868	48	A MEDICAL CORRESPONDENT	
E.D.M.	March 1869	49	TRY IT	
		51	AN OLD STAYWEARER	special letter from a male stay-wearer
E.D.M.	August 1868	56	A COLONEL	
		57	–	special letter from a girl seeking advice
		74	–	special letter – long account of a girl of eighteen's experiences of tight-lacing with the help of her aunt in Vienna.
E.D.M.	January 1868	81	A TIGHT-LACER	*The Corset and The Crinoline* p 168
E.D.M.	October 1867	82	MIGNONETTE	*The Corset and The Crinoline* p 149
E.D.M.	November 1867	83	DEBUTANTE	*The Corset and The Crinoline* p 150
E.D.M.	May 1867	83	NORA	*The Corset and The Crinoline* p 170
E.D.M.	February 1870	85	AGNES	
E.D.M.	July 1870	86	PERSEVERANCE	
E.D.M.	June 1870	88	MARY and AMY'S BROTHER	
E.D.M.	July 1870	90	ROBIN ADAIR	
E.D.M.	December 1870	92	PERSEVERANCE	
E.D.M.	July 1870	98	PERSEVERANCE	
E.D.M.	August 1868	100	M.C.	
E.D.M.	November 1867	105	EDINA	*The Corset and The Crinoline* p 192
		106	–	special letter re good health of tight-laced ladies.
		108	ROBIN ADAIR	special letter recommending Messrs Thomson's new *Curvilinear Corset* tried his sister's; also praises gymnastics for women.

From p109 onwards, the book deals with high heels and quotes the following letters:

Publication	Date	Page	Correspondent	
E.D.M.		113	unidentified	
London Society		113	unidentified article	I have not been able to trace
E.D.M.	September 1870	114	ROBIN ADAIR	praises high heels; specially on boots made by E.J. Nicoll, 424, Oxford Street; has some made for himself
E.D.M.	August 1870	118	SCIENCE AND ART	high heels depend on circumstances, not suitable for long walks
E.D.M.	December 1870	119	ROBIN ADAIR	various comments on 'chaussure' – prefers the 'demi-high button boot'.
		pages 121-125	describe a system of 'stocks' for the prevention of the turning-in of the toes: full details to be obtained from the London Stereoscopic Company, 110, Regent Street	There was correspondence about the use of stocks in E.D.M. January 1879, p55 June 1879 p330; July 1879, p54; and August 1879, p110

BIBLIOGRAPHY

A) OTHER CONTEMPORARY REFERENCES

Art of Beauty, or the best methods of improving and preserving the shape, carriage, etc.
(London: Knight and Lacey, 1825):
> I, The Beauty of the Shape and Carriage, pp 2-90.

Beale, Lionel John

The Laws of Health in relation to mind and body. A series of letters from an old practitioner to a patient
(London: John Churchill, 1851):
> Letter V: On the Organs and Functions of Respiration: mischief of tight dress and stays: pp. 45-8.

Caplin, Madame Roxey A.

Health and Beauty. First edition not in British Library, but press comments on her corsets date from 1843.

Health and Beauty; or, Corsets and Clothing, constructed in accordance with the Physiological laws of the human body. Second edition (London: Darton and Co, [1856]:
> iii, Opinions of the Press;
> Chapter V, The Corset, its History, Use and Abuse, pp. 35-41;
> Chapter VI, On the Adaptation of the Corset to the Body, pp. 42-51;
> Chapter IX, On Spinal Deformities, pp. 68-79
> (child bodice, 78-9).

Health and Beauty; or, Woman and her Clothing. Third edition (London: Kent and Co.,1864):
> Chapters as above;
> Appendix A. Madame Caplin's Inventions for the adaptation of the Dress to the Body etc. pp.175-80;
> Appendix B. Opinions of the Press [on Madame Caplin's Corsets], pp.181-193;
> Appendix C. Reviews of the Second edition, pp. 194-201.

Childs, G.B.

On the Improvement and Preservation of the Female Figure with a new mode of Treatment of Lateral Curvature of the Spine (London: Harvey and Darton, 1840):
> Section V. Injurious Effects of the present System of Education, etc., pp. 30-45;
> Section XVI. On the proper construction of Corsets: Mrs. Merriott, 3, Wigmore Street, pp.161-170.

Coulson, William

On Deformities of the Chest
(London: Thomas Hurst, 1836):
> Compression by Stays, pp. 46-70.

On Deformities of the Chest and Spine (1837). Missing in British Library.

On Deformities of the Chest and Spine, Second edition, greatly enlarged (London: Longman, Orme, Brown, Green and Longman, 1839):
> Sections XI - XVI, Stays, pp. 158-246.

Hare, Samuel

Practical Observations on the Causes and Treatment of Curvatures of the Spine
(London: Simpkin, Marshall & Co., 1838):
> Section II, On Impropriety of Dress, pp. 31-40.

Practical Observations etc. Second edition, Revised and Enlarged (London: John Churchill, 1844):
> Section II, On Impropriety of Dress, pp. 35-44.

Facts and Observations on the Physical Education of Children (London: J. Churchill, 1852):
> Dress, pp.22-41,
> Non-Compression Corsets, pp. 42-43.

Haweis, Mrs. H.R.

The Art of Beauty (London: Chatto & Windus, 1878):
> Stays and tight lacing: pp. 35, 48-51, 67-8, 120-22.

The Art of Dress (London: Chato & Windus, 1879):
> Tight lacing: pp.33-40.

Lynn, afterwards Linton, Elizabeth.

Ourselves. A series of essays on Women. Second edition (London, 1870).
A new edition (London: Chatto & Windus, 1884):
> "The Follies of Fashion," pp. 151-170.

Merrifield, Mrs.

Dress as a Fine Art
(London: Arthur Hall, Virtue & Co., 1854):
> Tight lacing: pp. 15-41,
> Children: pp. 118-122.

Tilt, Edward John.

On Diseases of Menstruation and Ovarian Inflammation etc. (London: John Churchill, 1850):
> The necessity for drawers, p.134.

Elements of Health and Principles of Female Hygiene (London: Henry G. Bohn, 1852):
> The best stays for children - Mrs. Caplin, Berners St. p. 143;
> The necessity for drawers, pp. 192-3;
> Stays, pp. 195-200.

Walker, Mrs. Alexander.

Female Beauty as preserved and improved by Regimen, Cleanliness and Dress etc. (London: Thomas Hurst, 1837):
> Part III Dress, Section II, Stays, pp. 310-333.

BIBLIOGRAPHY

B) SECONDARY SOURCES FOR THE PERIOD

Colmer, Michael

Whalebone to See-Through: A History of Body Packaging (London: Cassell, 1979)

Doyle, Robert

Waisted Efforts: An Illustrated Guide to Corset Making (Halifax, Nova Scotia: Sartorial Press Publications, 1997).

Farrer, Peter (editor)

Men in Petticoats: A Selection of Letters from Victorian Newspapers (Liverpool: Karn Publications Garston, 1987).

Borrowed Plumes: Letters from Edwardian Newspapers on Male Cross Dressing [includes early history of *The Queen*] (Liverpool: Karn publications Garston, 1994).

The Regime of the Stay-Lace: A Further Selection of Letters from Victorian Newspapers (Liverpool: Karn Publications Garston, 1995).

Fontanel, Beatrice

Support and Seduction: The History of Corsets and Bras (New York: Harry N. Abrams, 1997).

Kunzle, David

Fashion and Fetishism: A Social History of the Corset, Tight-Lacing and Other Forms of Body-Sculpture in the West (Totowa, New Jersey: Rowman and Littlefield, 1982).

Leoty, Ernest

Le Corset A Travers Les Ages (Paris: Paul Ollendorff, 1893).

Libron, F. and Clouzot, H.

Le Corset Dans L'Art et Les Moeurs du XIIIe au XXe Siecle (Paris, 1933).

Lord, William Barry

Freaks of Fashion: The Corset and the Crinoline (Reprinted Mendocino, California: R.L. Shep, 1993).

Page, Christopher

Foundations of Fashion: The Symington Collection: Corsetry from 1856 to the Present Day (Leicester: Leicestershire Museums. 1981).

Robinson, Julian

Body Packaging: A Guide to Sexual Display (London: Guild Publishing, 1988).

Secrets d'Elegance 1750-1950

Exhibition Catalogue, Musee de la Mode et du Costume, Palais Galliera, Paris, Dec. 1978 -April 1979.

Shep, R. L.

Corsets: A Visual History (Mendocino, California: R.L. Shep, 1993).
[Shep reprints the article in *The Penny Magazine*, 1833]

Steele, Valerie.

Fashion and Eroticism: Ideals of Feminine Beauty from the Victorian Era to the Jazz Age (New York and Oxford: O.U.P., 1985).

Fetish: Fashion, Sex and Power (New York and Oxford: O.U.P. 1996).

Waugh, Norah.

Corsets and Crinolines (London: B.T. Batsford, 1954. Reprinted New York: Routledge, Theater Arts Books, 1991).

Essential for research in this field are:

The British Union Catalogue of Periodicals, edited by J.D. Stewart, Muriel E. Hammond and Erwin Saenger (London: Butterworths Scientific Publications, 1954—) [gives location in U.K. libraries];

and

Poole's Index to Periodical Literature 1802-1881 by William Frederick Poole and William I. Fletcher (London: Kegan Paul, Trench, Trubner, 1882), with the successive Supplements.

MAKERS OR SUPPLIERS OF STAYS

For further information about corset makers, consult the Mactaggart's card index at The Gallery of Costume, Platt Hall.

REFERENCES TO MALE WEARERS

Family Herald:

29.4.1848, 12.1.1856, 16.1.1864.

Punch:

18.9.1869.

E.D.M.

4/1864, 11/1867, 5/1868, 6/1868, 7/1868. 8/1868, 9/1868, 10/1868, 11/1868, 12/1868, 1/1870, 12/1870, 1/1871, 3/1871, 4/1871, 6/1871, 7/1871, 8/1871, 9/1871, 5/1873.

S.H.J.

5/1878, 7/1879, 10/1879.

Dress.

p. 32

Figure Training

Appendix Four.